BIBLE TIME STORYBOOK

Stories of God's Love

This book belongs to

_____

from

_____

Chariot Books™

Here are stories of God's love, of how He created the world and protected a family He loved, of how God provided a place for a nation He loved and later sent His only son Jesus to Bethlehem because He loves us so much.

Illustrated by Bill Haines.
Written by Pat Palmer, Brenda G. Mutchnick, and John Barrett.
Originally published separately as *Creation, Noah, Joshua* and *The First Christmas.*

Chariot Books™ is an imprint of David C. Cook Publishing Co.
David C. Cook Publishing Co., Elgin, Illinois 60120
David C. Cook Publishing Co., Weston, Ontario
STORIES OF GOD'S LOVE
1976, 1990 by David C. Cook Publishing Co.
Cover and interior design by Dawn Lauck

First Printing, 1990
Printed in
94 93 92 91 90 5 4 3 2 1
 CIP applied for
The verses marked (TLB) are taken from The Living Bible© 1971, owned by assignment by the Illinois Regional Bank N.A. (as trustee). Used by permission of Tyndale House Publishers Inc., Wheaton, IL 60189. All rights reserved.

God Makes the World He Loves

The Story of Creation

Before God created the earth,
This was just an empty place,
Without a trace
Of things that you and I know.
There was no land,
Not one grain of sand
Where you and I stand,
There was no place to go.

There were no boys or girls,
Or flowers or trees,
No fish, no birds, no chimpanzees,
No macaroni and cheese, no Summer breeze,
There were no puppies, no guppies,
No pink lemonade,
It must have been lonely,
Before the earth was made.

So God formed a mighty plan,
And the creation of the world began.
He started by making light,
Then He separated light from what wasn't bright
And He called the light day,
And when day went away,
We had night.
Right?
It makes sense to me—what do you say?

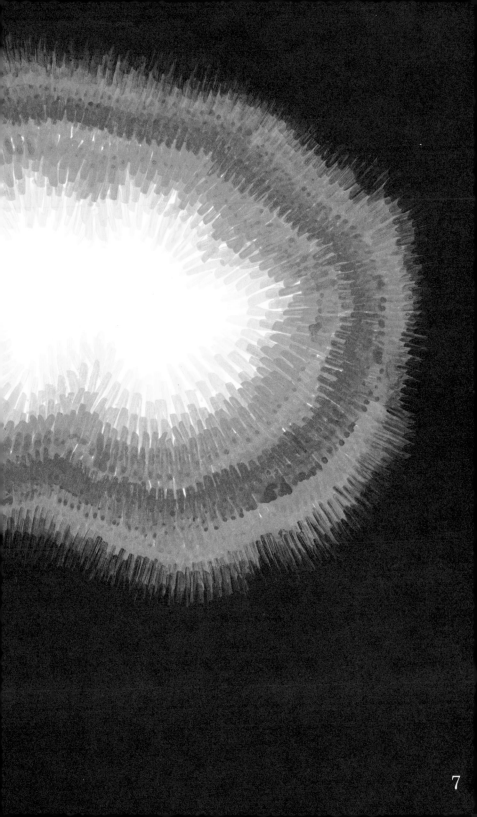

Then God began to work with care,
To separate the water and air,
And sure enough,
The sea grew rough,
And the sky above grew blue.
He had no sooner begun,
Than the job was done.
But God said, "I have more work to do."

"I'll make mountains and islands rise from the sea
In order that there then can be,
Dry land—where I can spend hours,
Making the plants and the trees and the flowers."

God made the stars and the moon and the sun,
He set them in motion and watched them all run,
He planned all of this for a special reason,
You see...

The days made weeks,
And the months made seasons;
Spring and Summer, Winter and Fall,
And God was happy with it all.

13

Then God filled the sea and the sky,
With fish that swim and birds that fly.
There were catfish and eels and bass,
And sharks,
And swallows and bobbin' head robins
And larks,
There were owls and eagles,
And parrots and quail,
Tuna and salmon,
And magnificent whales.

Next, God made animals...
Monkeys, dogs and pussycats,
Buffalo, bears and little white rats,
Turtles, reindeer and hippopotamuses,
Raccoons, sheep and rhinocerouses.
More than you'd ever see in a zoo.
Oh, did I forget the kangaroo?

17

God looked at His work and thought it was gran
The living things, the sea and the land,
He said,
"I wish there was a creature who appreciated
This beautiful world that I have created."

And God formed a plan.
He molded clay with care
To resemble Himself.
He breathed in life and said,
"There
Is the very first man."

And the man was called Adam.

And God said, "Adam, I am going to give
You a special place in which to live.
It's a garden and it will be your duty,
To look after the place and all of its beauty."

God put Adam in the wonderful land
Called Eden and Adam began
To grow carrots and oranges,
Walnuts and wheat,
Potatoes, tomatoes—good things to eat.

There were trees tall and shapely,
Appley and mapley,
And bananas by the bunch.
Fine evergreens, peas, beans,
More than enough for lunch.

Only Adam was lonely.

21

And God said, "Yes, I can see,
Adam needs some company.
I think I will bring the animals here,
You can talk with the tigers
And chat with the deer."

Into the garden the animals came,
And Adam gave them each a name.
The chickens and horses romped about,
And the bumblebees tried to help Adam out.

Adam said, "The animals are happy,
And the plants have grown some,
But, to tell you the truth, I still feel lonesome.
I've tried talking to animals in this new wonderlan
But visiting with lizards—
Well, they just don't understand."

Adam needed a friend, someone who could lend
A helping hand and stand by him in this new land

So Adam went to sleep.

When Adam awakened,
He found God had taken
One of the ribs from his side,
And with careful measure
God fashioned a treasure,
"It's a woman," Adam cried.

Adam and Eve were very excited,
They came before God and He was delighted.
He said, "This earth is yours to love and care for,
That is exactly what I put you there for."

Adam and Eve became man and wife,
They married and started a beautiful life,
And God said, "Have no secrets, be not afraid,
Everything is perfect in all that I've made."

And God said, "You'll never be alone,
Because you have each other.
Now I want you to become,
The very first father and mother."

Which is precisely why,
You see,
You became you and
I became me.

Do you remember the last time you looked at a flower? Maybe it was red. Or perhaps it was yellow or white or blue. Was it tall or short? Big or little? What did it smell like?

Who made the flowers?

Do you like animals? How many can you name on pages 16 and 17?

God made the animals.
How should we take care of what He created?

What can we do to take better care of the world God created?

Look at your hand. Close your hand —
s-l-o-w-l-y. Open and close it quickly!!!
Do it again and again.
Touch your thumb to each finger, one at a
time. What else can your wonderful hand do?

Who made your hand?
Who made wonderful
you?

"Adam and Eve
were very excited.
They came before
God and He was
delighted."
Isn't it wonderful
that God is delighted
in you and delighted in
me? And isn't it
wonderful that He loves us?

T H E   B I B L E   S A Y S —

See how much our heavenly
Father loves us.

1 JOHN 3:3
Taken from *The Illustrated Bible* (TLB)

God loved what He created. And Adam and Eve loved God, until one awful, terrible, horrible day when Adam and Eve decided that they knew better than God, and they disobeyed Him.

God forgave Adam and Eve, but the world was never perfect again. And after many, many years, the world was in a terrible state—except for one family that still obeyed God.

God loved Noah and God loved Noah's family. Here is the amazing story of how God protected Noah and his family through the very worst flood ever.

God Protects a Family He Loves

The Story of Noah and the Ark

Things were in a terrible state.
No one was behaving.
It almost broke the poor Lord's heart.
The world was not worth saving.

There lived one man, however,
  who was as good as good can be.
His name was Noah. His age, a hundred
  times six — you see.

Now the Lord told Noah all about his plan.
And how disappointed he had been in the
  behavior of man.
And how soon He would destroy everything
From the creatures on the earth
  and those that have wings.

But because Noah had always led such
  a good life,
The Lord would spare him, his sons,
  and all their wives.

Noah listened carefully to all the Lord's
    directions.
Things would have to be perfect—
    there could be no corrections.

So he built an ark made of gopher wood.
And he and his sons worked as hard
    as they could.

Because in seven more days it would start
to rain.
So Noah sat with his wife and began
to explain,
"All the world will be covered by
a very great flood.
That means lots of water and it
means lots of mud."

And he told her to make a list of
all the things
The Lord had said to be sure to bring.
So she sat with her list at the door
of the ark
And checked them all off from
dawn until dark.

44

"We have two of all creatures who creep
    on the ground.
We have two of all birds who fly all around.
We have two of each animal—clean and
    unclean.
And have two of some things that I've
    never seen."

"I placed all the food in packets and jars.
This side for animals— and this side is ours.
Now hurry along,
    this is not the time to fight.
Don't keep the Lord waiting—
    that's quite impolite."

And when they all became settled
The Lord shut the door.
And for forty days and forty nights
The rain continued to pour.

Water fell from the sky.
And from the earth rose mighty fountains.
'Til every single tree was covered
And even all the mountains.

Noah and his sons, Japeth, Ham and Shem
Were busy stopping leaks from
    stern to stem.
And all of the wives were kept really busy
Just feeding the animals without getting dizzy.

The lightning and the thunder
    continued to roar.
And the rain, it kept raining—
    it just continued to pour.

And after sailing on the ark for 150-days,
The Lord sent some soft winds
   to make the waters go away.
And then one day the ark suddenly stopped
And rested on mountains called Ararat.

51

There was quite a commotion
     inside the ark.
The sheep got so silly,
     they all started to bark.
The monkeys were restless
     and wanted to play,
While the bumblebees kept
     on buzzing all the long day.

"Noah dear," his wife exclaims,
"What do you want for dinner?
  And something special
     for the elephants.
     They're skinny.
     They're looking thinner.
  And yesterday
     my peacocks would
     not touch a crumb.
  And the bears just lay
     in bed all day and tried
     to suck their thumbs."

53

So they just sat there three months
    and forty more days,
While the water kept on going down
    a long, long ways.
Then Noah opened the window a tiny
    little crack
And sent out a dove—but it soon
    flew right back.

They let another week go by.
And Noah again asked the dove to fly.
And when she brought back the branch
   of a tree,
They knew there'd soon be land to see.

57

But to make absolutely sure that
   the earth was dry,
They stayed inside the ark and
   many days went by.

And finally Noah opened the door
   nice and wide
And yelled down the halls,
   "Everybody! You can all come outside."

For they'd been cooped up now
   for almost a year,
And that's just about more than
   a grown-up can bear.

59

The Lord met them at the ark
   and with a warm and joyful smile.
He was happy to see them—
   it had been quite a while.
"Thank you, Dear Lord," said Noah,
   "For bringing us safely here.
And thank you, Dear Lord,
   for watching over us during the year."

And then the Lord said, "I will never again
Bring a flood of that kind to the
   women and men.
And now all of you who have sailed
   on the waters
Be fruitful of the land—have more sons
   and daughters."

61

And the Lord said, "Noah—look up there high—
I have put a rainbow into the sky.
And whenever that rainbow appears,
    now and then,
It's a promise the earth won't be destroyed
    by water again."

Then everyone got busy—
    there was so much work to do
To get the world ready—
    for me and for you.

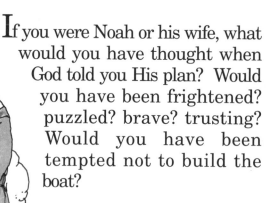

If you were Noah or his wife, what would you have thought when God told you His plan? Would you have been frightened? puzzled? brave? trusting? Would you have been tempted not to build the boat?

Think about building a huge boat the size of a football field. Remember, Noah and his sons did not have electric saws or drills. They had to saw every board by hand. What would you say to your dad at the end of a long, hot day of sawing and hammering? And, if you were Noah, what would you have told your three sons about loving and obeying God?

Think about when you went to the zoo or visited a farm. What was the biggest animal you saw? What was the smallest? Which was your favorite animal? Imagine that you are Noah or Mrs. Noah watching the animals, and pretend that you are directing the animals where to go. Why would you be happy that you obeyed God and built the boat?

In our first story God created the animals and people. Now He saved them because He loved Noah and Noah loved Him. Noah said, "Thank you, dear Lord, for watching over us during the year." Do you think God can protect you, too? Ask somebody to tell about a time when he or she was protected from a serious injury.

THE BIBLE SAYS —

I cannot count the times when you have faithfully rescued me from danger. I will tell everyone how good you are, and of your constant, daily care.

PSALM 71:15
Taken from The Illustrated Bible (TLB)

After a whole year on a ship, how would you have felt when Noah yelled, "Everyone! You can all go outside." Would you have said, "I thought this journey would never end?"

Many, many years later another group of people called Israelites were on a long journey. In fact, they had traveled for forty straight years. Do you think the Israelites were ready for the journey to end? The Israelites were very special people, because God had chosen to love them in a very wonderful way. Through this nation Jesus would someday be born.

The Israelites had been slaves in Egypt, but God had promised to give them a country called Caanan. After all their traveling they were ready to enter this Promised Land. But first, they needed to cross a wide river and destroy the evil, God-hating city of Jericho. This story tells how God provided a home for the Israelites, a people He loved. Joshua was their leader, and he and his people loved God and obeyed God.

God Provides a Home for People He Loves

The Story of Joshua and the Walls of Jericho

Joshua led his people through
The dusty desert waste.
Then one night the Israelites felt
A cool wind in their face.

Far beyond their camp was the river Jordan
And a country that was cool and green.
The tribes of wandering Israelites said,
"That's the prettiest land we have seen!"

"That's the land of Caanan," Joshua said,
"And it's going to be our home.
God has promised us that land so we won't
Have to roam."

He was strong and brave; and the good Lord
Gave Joshua his command.

"Obey my word, and I'll deliver you across
That river to the Promised Land."

Joshua pointed off in the distance. He said,
"There's where we must go!"
Far across the Jordan on a towering hill
Was the city of Jericho.

"It's a wicked city," said Joshua, "and it's
Going to feel God's wrath.
For there's only one way to the Promised Land
And Jericho guards the path."

Joshua said, "In six more days, we'll do as
God has planned,
We'll cross that river and take that city
And claim the Promised Land!"

69

Joshua called for volunteers: "I need two good
Men to scout.
Now I want you guys to act as spies and check
That fortress out!"

"Go to that city in the dead of night and check
Those towering walls.
For in a few more days, our army moves and
That fortress city falls!"

The spies made their way across the raging
River and slipped through the city gate.
They quietly moved along the mighty walls
And began to investigate.

"This wall," said one, "is awful tall!"
Said the other, "Yeah, and it's just as thick!"
The pair heard soldiers approaching and said,
"We'd better get out of here quick!"

The spies hurried to an open door and ducked
Inside an inn to hide.

The room they found was dimly lit, and a
Woman stood inside.

"I know why you're here, there's no need to
Fear, come in," the woman said.
"I'll help you escape back to Joshua's camp.
If you're caught in here, you're dead!"

"Go hide on the roof, and wait for my call
But hurry, don't delay!
I'll tell those troops that are searching the
Wall that you went the other way."

"But," said the woman, "when you attack,
Please remember me.
When the Army of God destroys this city,
Pray spare my family."

Back in the camp, Joshua stood and spoke
To the Israelites:
"Tomorrow," he said, "we march to that river,
And there we begin God's fight."

"Listen to all that God has said — let no man
Have a doubt,
For tomorrow will begin a miracle that will
Surely drive our enemies out."

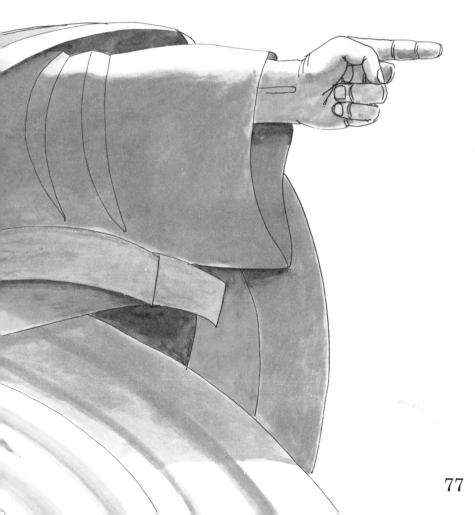

The morning dawned, and Joshua stood by the
River Jordan's side.
"I want the priests to step in the water and
Move against the tide."

The priests picked up the Ark of God,
Joshua said, "March on!"
Their feet touched the edge of the fast-flowing
River, and suddenly the water was gone.

Joshua watched the water disappear where
The Israelite priests had trod.
He said, "That's proof that the Children of
Israel worship a living God!"

Joshua turned to his awe-struck tribes and
Issued a proud command:
"Walk in the path where the river used to be
And set foot in the Promised Land!"

When one and all had made the crossing,
The river filled its banks.
Joshua knelt in prayer before his people
And said, "Let us give thanks."

"For the God who performed this miracle
And made the Jordan cease to flow
Is the God who will help us take those walls
Surrounding Jericho."

Joshua made camp and spoke with his spies,
Studied maps of the city on the hill.
"Tomorrow morning, as the sun arises,
My troops will do God's will."

"Here's God's plan," said Joshua.
"At the first light of the morn,

Seven priests will circle the city and start
Blowing on Jehovah ram horns."

"The Army of Israel will quietly guard,
But shall not raise a sword!
We're here to show the city of Jericho.
The mighty power of the Lord!"

83

So the morning came and in God's name,
Joshua's troops assembled.
And the priests marched out and blew their horns,
And the people of Jericho trembled.

The commander of the garrison at Jericho
Cried, "Why don't they attack?"
"Why any other army would have stormed our gates
And my men might have driven them back."

"But instead, they march around the walls,
Out of the range of spears.
And that dreadful sound of those mournful horns
Fills my men with fear!"

Joshua marched around the walls one time
And then turned to his men:
"Let's make camp now, for tomorrow morning
We'll do it all again."

For six whole days Joshua marched
His troops 'round the fortress walls.
And the people in the city shivered at the sight
And the sound of the trumpet call.

On the seventh day, Joshua said, "We'll
Show those Caananites.
The God Who marches with Israel
Today will end our fight!"

Then Joshua said, "Don't say a word
Until I tell you to…"
So the Children of Israel began to march,
And the sound of those trumpets grew.

On the seventh day, seven times Joshua's
Troops did go,
And as they circled the city, for the seventh time,
They felt God's power grow.

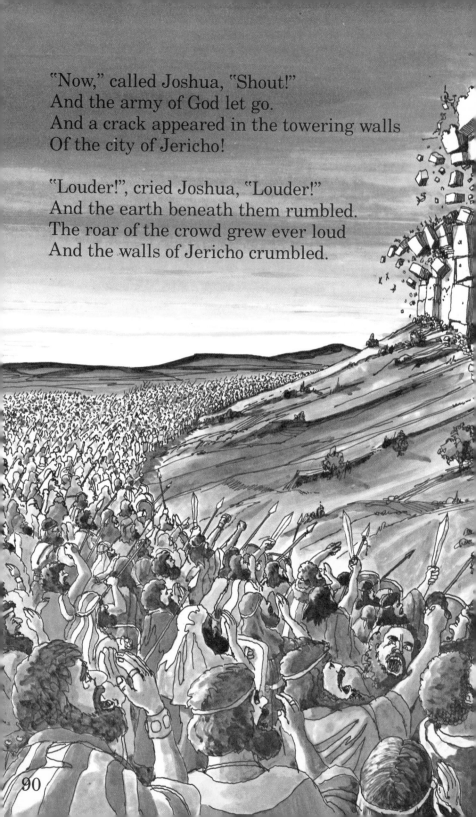

"Now," called Joshua, "Shout!"
And the army of God let go.
And a crack appeared in the towering walls
Of the city of Jericho!

"Louder!", cried Joshua, "Louder!"
And the earth beneath them rumbled.
The roar of the crowd grew ever loud
And the walls of Jericho crumbled.

The Army of Israel poured through the ruins
And yelled triumphantly.
Joshua called to his troops to remember
To spare one family.

"Destroy the city," Joshua said,
"Everyone must die!"
"Except the woman and her family
Who helped and protected my spies!"

It was a long time ago at Jericho
And that victory of the Israelites.
And the ruins of that city still tell the tale
Of Joshua's famous fight.

Joshua marched in where other men
Might have been afraid.

For he and his people had faith in the Lord
And one God that they obeyed.

People still sing about Joshua
A story of long ago.
When he won fame and glory to the name
Of God at Jericho.

Have you ever sung the old song "Joshua fought the Battle of Jericho, and the walls came tumbling down"?

But first Joshua and the Israelites had to get to Jericho. How would you feel if you were a priest and Joshua had told you to walk to the edge of the river and keep on walking?

After you got to the other side of the river, what would you have prayed to God? What would you have told your friend about God's power to take down the walls of Jericho?

1. Once
2. Once
3. Once
4. Once
5. Once
6. Once

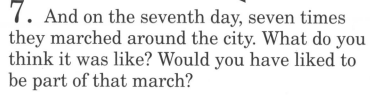

7. And on the seventh day, seven times they marched around the city. What do you think it was like? Would you have liked to be part of that march?

Do you ever watch spy movies? The stories can be exciting and sometimes scary. What would it have been like to be one of the spies who went to Jericho? Would it have been difficult or easy to keep trusting God for safety?

Who promised a very special land to a people He loved?

Who dried up the Jordan River?

Who caused the walls of Jericho to fall?

Who always keeps His promises?

THE BIBLE SAYS—

They did not conquer by their own strength and skill, but by your mighty power and because you smiled upon them and favored them.

PSALM 44:3
Taken from *The Illustrated Bible* (TLB)

The woman who helped the two spies at Jericho was a very important woman. Not only did she assist Joshua in capturing the city, but she became part of the family tree of Jesus. Because she loved and obeyed God, her family became very special. Did you know that God thinks you are special, too?

God thinks you are so special that He decided to send Jesus to a town a few miles from where Joshua crossed the river. So, many, many years after God created Adam and Eve and after He saved Noah and after Joshua entered the Promised  Land, Joseph and Mary lived in a small village of Nazareth. They loved God and wanted to obey Him. God knew that they would be just the right parents for Jesus, the Promised One who would save us from our sins.

God Sends Jesus Because He Loves Us

The Story of Christmas

The Christmas Story
Is a tale of glory—
A story of wonder and joy
About God, who gave
His Son to save
Every girl and boy.

The story began
With a woman and man.
Their names were Joseph and Mary.
Both of them loved
The Lord above,
And soon they would be married.

Then an angel's voice
Said, "Mary, rejoice.
For I have come to proclaim:
You will bear God's Son,
The Promised One,
And Jesus shall be His name."

At first she was frightened,
Then Mary brightened
At the angel's glorious word.
Happily,
Lovingly,
She told Joseph what she had heard.

Joseph refused
To believe the news.
It was clear that he wasn't pleased.
But an angel came
In a dream to explain
And put Joseph's mind at ease.

Then all Galilee
Received a decree
From Caesar, the ruler in Rome.
The order directed
A tax be collected
In the town each person called home.

As the story is told,
The weather was cold
For outside the winter winds blew.
The journey was long,
And Mary not strong
For the little Baby was due.

The pair set out
On a journey South
For the taxes had to be paid.
Weather blown,
They traveled alone
On a road on a cold winter's day.

It was necessary
That Joseph and Mary
Follow Caesar's command.
But did they know,
On that road long ago,
That God had set out to save man?

The journey took them
To Bethlehem,
The town where Joseph was born.
They looked on the way
For a place they could stay
For Mary was cold and worn.

"There are no beds,"
The innkeeper said.
"There's nothing I can suggest."
Joseph frowned.
"My wife must lie down.
We've come far, and she needs to rest."

Joseph's words caused
The innkeeper to pause
And look at the dusty stranger.
"A baby, you say?
Well, perhaps she should stay
With the animals back in the manger?"

"It's the best I can do,"
He said, taking them to
Where the manger was located.
So Mary was able
To lie in the stable.
And Joseph and Mary waited.

Midnight,
Starlight,
Bethlehem has gone to sleep.
God will bring
His Son, the King
To earth, midst cattle and sheep.

Midnight,
Starlight,
The Bethlehem night has grown chill.
The Baby arrives,
God's Son is alive!
For a moment, the whole world stands still.

While Bethlehem slept,
In the hills, shepherds kept
Watch on their sheep nearby.
The night grew bright
With a heavenly light,
And an angel appeared in the sky.

"I bring to you
Glorious news!"
And the angel told of the birth
Of a Savior, a King,
A Man who would bring
Salvation and peace on earth.

The shepherds fell to their knees,
And said "Tell us please.
Where can we worship Him?"
The Angel said.
"Well, He hasn't a bed,
He's in a manger in Bethlehem."

As the shepherds drew near,
More angels appeared,
And the night air fairly glistened.
The lonely hills rang
With the song they sang,
And the breathless shepherds listened.

With what they had learned,
The shepherds turned
And down the hillside they ran.
Worshipfully,
They said, "We must see
God's Son who was born as a Man."

In the manger in town,
The shepherds found
The place where the Baby lay.
The only sound,
For miles around,
Was the animals' soft serenade.

123

The shepherds told Joseph and Mary
Of the extraordinary
Sight that they had seen...
Of the heavenly throng,
And the angels' song.
And Mary looked very serene.

The shepherds then gazed
In loving praise
At the Baby who lay there and smiled.
Then slowly knelt
By the manger and felt
The love of the little Child.

With the shepherds enthralled,
Mary recalled
The words when the angel first came.
With appropriate prayer,
The parents prepared
To give the Baby His name.

Christmas began
When God gave man
His Son, our Savior and King.
On this Christmas Eve,
With the gifts you receive,
Think of the gift only Jesus can bring.

Christmas happened because God not only loved Adam and Eve and Noah and his family and Joshua and the Israelites, but because He loves each of us and wants to give us the gift of Jesus.

What's the biggest gift you ever received? The most fun gift? The most important gift?

Do you remember the very last gift you gave? What was it? Do you enjoy giving gifts? Try to remember a very special time when you gave just the right gift to someone who is special to you.

How do you think God feels about that special time when her gave us Jesus? Do you think that is why He wants us to love Jesus?

THE BIBLE SAYS —

"And she will have a Son, and you shall name him Jesus (meaning 'Savior'), for he will save his people from their sins."

MATTHEW 1:21

Taken from *The Illustrated Bible* (TLB)